*Old Woman with Berries in Her Lap*

## Alaska Literary Series

PEGGY SHUMAKER, SERIES EDITOR

The Alaska Literary Series publishes poetry, fiction, and literary nonfiction. Successful manuscripts have a strong connection to Alaska or the circumpolar north, are written by people living in the far north, or both. We prefer writing that makes the northern experience available to the world, and we choose manuscripts that offer compelling literary insights into the human condition.

*Armor and Ornament* by Christopher Lee Miles

*Be-Hooved* by Mar Ka

*Benchmarks* by Richard Dauenhauer

*Cabin, Clearing, Forest* by Zach Falcon

*Cabin 135* by Katie Eberhart

*The City Beneath the Snow* by Marjorie Kowalski Cole

*Cold Latitudes* by Rosemary McGuire

*Cold Spell* by Deb Vanasse

*The Cormorant Hunter's Wife* by Joan Kane

*The Creatures at the Absolute Bottom of the Sea* by Rosemary McGuire

*Ends of the Earth* by Kate Partridge

*Gaining Daylight* by Sara Loewen

*The Geography of Water* by Mary Emerick

*Human Being Songs* by Jean Anderson

*I Follow in the Dust She Raises* by Linda Martin

*In the Quiet Season and Other Stories* by Martha Amore

*Just Between Us* by David McElroy

*A Ladder of Cranes* by Tom Sexton

*Leavetakings* by Corinna Cook

*Li Bai Rides a Celestial Dolphin Home* by Tom Sexton

*Of Darkness and Light* by Wendy Erd

*Oil and Water* by Mei Mei Evans

*Old Woman with Berries in Her Lap* by Vivian Faith Prescott

*Overwinter* by Jeremy Pataky

*The Rabbits Could Sing* by Amber Flora Thomas

*River of Light* by John Morgan and Kesler Woodward

*Roughly for the North* by Carrie Ayagaduk Ojanen

*Sailing by Ravens* by Holly J. Hughes

*Spirit Things* by Lara Messersmith-Glavin

*Threadbare* by Mary Kudenov

*Upriver* by Carolyn Kremers

*Water Mask* by Monica Devine

*Water the Rocks Make* by David McElroy

*Whiteout* by Jessica Goodfellow

*Wild Rivers, Wild Rose* by Sarah Birdsall

# Old Woman with Berries in Her Lap

POEMS BY

## Vivian Faith Prescott

ALASKA LITERARY SERIES

University of Alaska Press
*Fairbanks*

© 2022 by University Press of Colorado

Published by University of Alaska Press
An imprint of University Press of Colorado
245 Century Circle, Suite 202
Louisville, Colorado 80027

All rights reserved
Manufactured in the United States of America

The University Press of Colorado is a proud member
of Association of University Presses.

The University Press of Colorado is a cooperative publishing enterprise
supported, in part, by Adams State University, Colorado State University,
Fort Lewis College, Metropolitan State University of Denver, University of
Alaska, University of Colorado, University of Northern Colorado, University
of Wyoming, Utah State University, and Western Colorado University.

∞ This paper meets the requirements of the ANSI/
NISO Z39.48–1992 (Permanence of Paper).

ISBN: 978-1-60223-453-6 (paperback)
ISBN: 978-1-60223-454-3 (ebook)
https://doi.org/10.5876/9781602234543

Cataloging-in-Publication data for this title is available online at the Library of Congress.

Cover photograph, "The construction of Sami tent—
north Norway," © VojtechVlk/Shutterstock.

*To the North American Sámi Community*

To our elders and yoikers, scholars, historians,
scientists, and activists. To our noiades and
knowledge bearers, and to our teachers and
seekers. To the language learners, and to our
poets, writers, musicians, and storytellers.
To our duodji crafters, artists, and medicine
makers. To all who make up or our Sámi
diaspora—through our shared báiki, may
our community continue to thrive.

Sámi Riddle: *What is an old woman with berries in her lap?*
Answer: *A well-traveled lavvu with a fire in the center.*

# Contents

UNRAVEL THE WIND

TRAVELING TO THE SUN

A DARK IMAGINING

THE TENT WALL STILL BREATHES

# Acknowledgments

Gunalchéesh, Shtax'héen Kwáan, for the opportunity to live at my fish-camp in Kaachxaana.áak'w, Wrangell, near Keishangita.aan. I'm a guest in Tlingit Aaní and I write these words on your precious land.

I would like to thank the Rasmuson Foundation (Individual Artist Award/Fellowships, 2015 and 2019), the Alaska State Council on the Arts (ASCA), and Peggy Shumaker and Joe Usibelli (Alaska Literary Award, 2017) for providing the time and means to complete this manuscript. I am grateful to the North American Sámi community members: Pacific Samí Searvi, Saami Baiki, Samí Cultural Center of North America, and the Saami North American Issues Forum, among others. I would also like to thank the University Press of Colorado for their support and expertise.

Thank you to everyone at the University of Alaska Press: editor Peggy Shumaker and Director Nate Bauer, plus UA Press's invaluable support staff. Thank you to the advisory board, reviewers, and everyone who believed this poetry collection was a good fit for the Alaska Literary Series. Also, I'm grateful to Joeth Zucco's copyediting expertise and Kristina Kachele Design for crafting a work of literary art.

Thank you to the many journals and chapbooks where my work first appeared. Some of the poems were published under different titles.

*Alaska Women Speak*: "Our tents are small volcanoes," "Exhibit 422: The Shaman's Drum," "*Gaska-geardi*—Layer of crust," "*Skoavdi*—Empty space," "*Bihci*—Rime," "*Doali*—Road or track covered by snow, but still distinguishable," and "*Jovagama*—Deep snow that lies undisturbed and does not get blown away"

*A-Minor Magazine*: "*Fáskka*—Snow blown by the wind into an embankment"

*Cascadia: A Literary Field Guide*: "*Šalka*—Firm, hard, winter way; hard-trodden snow on yard, a marked-place"

*Cirque*: "The Fire Tender"

*Drunken Boat*, First Peoples Issue: "Cartography" and "Check the Box"

*Glass: A Journal of Poetry*: "*Ukiuq*—Become winter"

*Great Weather for MEDIA* anthology: "Check the Box" and "Drawing Blanks"

*Mud City Journal*: "Google Saami"

*Spillway*: "*Vuožži*—Wet bare ice"

*Tidal Echoes*: "*Rodda*—Hard going (too little snow)," and "*Srevlla*—The state of things where the spring snow is so soft that one sinks into it"

*Yellow Medicine Review*: "*Jolas*—Tracks made in the snow," "*Beallgalmmas*—Half-frozen," and "Write like a Sámi"

Drum symbols on title page and poem "Observant" hand drawn by author, inspired by paintings on historical Sámi noiade drums

Collage title "Observant" from Kristian Emil Shreiner, painting by Astri Wellhaven Heiberg (1949)

"Observations of the Lapp Jaw," "Google Saami," "Our skulls are filled with suns," "Cartography," "How to say IT," "*Vuohttit*—To observe and learn from tracks" (originally published as "Archives"), "Unleash," "Stolen by Colonizers: Google Search for Our Sámi Drums," "Write Like a Sámi," "All the Sámi Findings," "Check the Box," "Anthroapology," "Observant," "Remedy for Assimilation," appeared in the chapbook *Traveling with the Underground People* (Finishing Line Press, 2017)

"Sonnet for Migrations," "*Vuohttit*—To observe and learn from tracks," "Transgenerationalmigrationallinguisticalgenocidalinaudible historicalvernacular," "*Njáhcu*—Thaw," "Our tents are small volcanoes," "*Earpmi*—A little snowfall where the snowflakes are very small," "*Oavlluš*—Depression or hollow with slushy snow in it, on land or on ice," "*Spildi*—Very thin layer of ice on water or milk" (originally published as "Yoik"), "Exhibit 422: The Shaman's Drum," "Likewise Great Observers of Omens," "*Guoldu*—Cloud of snow blowing up from the ground," "Drawing Blanks," "*Rodda*—Hard going (too little snow)," "In the Age of Print," appeared in the chapbook *Our Tents Are Small Volcanoes* (Quills Edge Press, 2017)

The manuscript *Old Woman with Berries in Her Lap* was a finalist for the 2018 Snyder Prize.

*Old Woman with Berries in Her Lap*

# She Was Taught How to Be Born

Her elders said—Feel for
branches, breathe snow.

# Our tents are small volcanoes

The center of our cosmos moves, our fire falls inward,
our boats are filled to the brim, ready to migrate again.

*my foot presses the gas pedal on the old truck.*

We move the birch floor. Find lost fragments of bone,
sewing needles. We sweep away our footprints, light
birch-branch fires. Nothing must remain. Nothing.

*the rusty grocery cart clunks down the aisle.*
*Inside it, my baby sleeps in her yellow plastic cradle.*

We row and splash, pole over stones. dogs bay and
children cry. someone chants.

*one package of macaroni, one large can*
*of tomato soup, baby formula. i unfold*
*the grocery list, cross off things*
*i haven't yet put in the cart. most things*

Summer clothes are in the storehouse. We take out winter gear:
parkas and tunics, a silver belt. We unpack our winter shoes,
dried reindeer meat.

*in the middle of aisle 3, i enter a space, hold tight*
*to the rim of this trail long since disappeared.*
*the vanishing point appears and disappears.*
*the boxed cereal tumbles from the shelf.* And I brush
willow branches aside. My baby cradles atop the reindeer pack.
In the distance I see gold firelight inside the tents.

Shadows move across its taut skin, women tend fires;
a child is enfolded in a fur blanket.

> *afterward, after the fire fades, after the underground people*
> *return home, and i pay for my groceries with a fistful of silver coins,*
>
> *i pull the truck over at city park, lean against the door,*
> *and light a cigarette. my baby girl fusses in her cradle*
> *and i recall my elders saying fire draws people together,*
>
> *pulls our stories from our bellies. this i know to be true—*
> *my baby is hungry and i search the horizon for small volcanoes.*

*If we add other related terms (verbs and adjectives), and if we include all possible derivations, we may probably very easily come up to something like one thousand lexemes with connections to snow, ice, freezing, and melting.*

~ Ole Henrik Magga

## *Rodda*—Hard going (too little snow)

Because you believe in rain
you stand outside and shake

a brass rattle and the clouds darken.
Elders tell me reindeer are happy when clouds

pull down to tundra—rain
drives away mosquitoes.

Tell me, how will you change the weather
without a shaman?

Teach me to become rain.

# A Thousand Words for Snow

And what of the old ones
who walked out of the lavvu alone
with only a thin deer hide to lay upon the tundra.

It was a good night, star-cindered and cold.
He lay there, fleece frosting his eyelids
watching northern lights, awaiting his ancestors.

When he still recalled his dreams,
he told me how the world was melting,
but no one can imagine

  *ratti skoarádat suovdnji šuohmir*

  *the absence of our footprints,*

how the tundra flowers press into bog
with the sting of snow's memory.

  On this cold night he evoked the words:

  *Winter way made by driving reindeer (in harness) over the snow.*

  *The kind of going in which one hears a grating noise as the sleigh
  or skis pass over a rough surface.*

  *Grazing hole dug by reindeer in the snow.*

  *Particle of ice in the shape of a needle . . .*

# In the Age of Print

We entered the European consciousness

like frost furrowing deep
into silence—
a shrine of wind.

He served as priest, diplomat, explorer.
He feared mosquitos and snow and us.

An unnamable voice
pulls space over
our outstretched arms. We chant each other.

Our landscape and peoples—a wonderland
of marvels and botanicals.

Everything was claimed and taxed:
three reindeer skins per Sámi.

We were portrayed and researched,
studied and framed.

And declared a great wilderness,
a natural man, unfettered, like wild beasts.

Exotic. The first Arcticus.

Open your eyes now.
There are ghosts in every direction.

*Seanas*—The dry, large-grained, and water-holding snow at the deepest layers, closest to the ground surface, found in late winter and spring; it is easy for reindeer to dig through *seanas*

---

I keep a secret—
I can hold water and travel on snow.
I will survive related terms, possible derivations,

a thousand lexemes, connections to snow,
ice freezing and melting. I can expect the chill,
be thawed, rid myself of adhering ice.

Some days, though, words don't form,
and if they do, they're swept up in clouds
of snow from the ground.

But some days the rise and fall of my landscape
is the bodyscape remembering
like those who dance in winter.

I've been practicing dancing on this
narrow strip of ice, on the snow bridge over rivers,
along the shore of open water,

against pack ice pressed to the riverbank.

# Beallgalmmas—Half-frozen

*To my ancestors who left their migratory life and to those who stayed.*

That first meeting of our faint tracks
    you called me out from

the line drawn in water,
    leaving wind pressing earth,

keeping it close to the deepest lake.
    My presence reminded you

that you could've been more
    like us—an unfurled breath,

a flight of spirit. But, no,
    you went packing,

took your children, pulling the whole
    of life into a strange form.

That day also brought you a village
    beneath a pocket of sky,

but it slipped into the lake
    before your eyes

and you wondered if your mind
    was tricking you until the wind

gave you instructions—stay back
    and dream of our singing.

# Cartography

Grandmother, you chewed alder
to red paste, mixed ash from woodstoves,

a tincture traced on swollen bellies,
landmarks for reindeer traveling to the sun—

charcoal figures: fisher and boat, hunter's bow,
a conduit between skydome and tundra.

You warmed painted hide by camplight
in the season before black robes silenced

our trances. Now, I peer at drummed bellies
beneath a tree rising from the center,

our sun-skins now mute behind museum glass.
What remains is now hidden on mountains

near seiddas—rock piles, beneath sedge.
Though, I still see your patterns moving

upon lavvu walls, sketching tracks to the pulse
of thumb, hooves on the rim of my drum,

a map lingering with lichen-scent, signposts
herding my migration toward home.

# *Vuohttit*—To observe and learn from tracks

I cling to old maps,
braided rivers, deep blue lakes

read under half-moon lamps.

I hold
an aroma of memory—musty

and coffee stained. Words jotted here and there,

like footprints wandering over stones and roots.
I am not born of this world—
I am unmarked by this knowing.

# Drawing Blanks

*Sen kaikki kyllä huomasivat ettemme olleet valkoisia.*
*Everybody recognized that we were not white.* ~ Nils-Aslak Valkeapää

White Indigenous people are_____.

All Saami love reindeer because_____.

You aren't Indigenous because you don't live_____.

If you don't know how to yoik you are_____.

Drawing blanks is like shooting blanks is like being draped in fur blankets
at night. unlimited coverlet encased and overspreading the empty space.
you face your face. Blankety-Blankety-blank. That blank look wrapped
you and shot through you. You make a blanket statement.

If you think Santa Claus is the most widespread misappropriation
of culture in history you are _____.

You are Indigenous because_____.

Your ancestors lived in tipis because_____.

You have the urge to migrate because_____.

Your tongue is blank. You are quite. quiet. when the molecules in the room
refer to whiteness. Every day you sense your ladder twisting to a spiral.
Nothing is certain except when it is. As a kid you blanked out. Teachers
yelled at you for it. You still stare ahead and are frequently asked what is
the matter or what the matter is.

You are quiet when watching the northern lights because_____
_____.

You can't speak your native tongue because_____.

Shamanism is_____.

You are fascinated with the sun and wind because_____.

But matter is the matter and it is nothingness you migrate toward.
But you know matter is the histories we are made of. Void.

gap. break. empty space. erase. erase. erase. This trancelike state. Blank.
Fill it in. Instill it. Uninstall it. This uncomfortable skin you're in has
been colonized for hundreds of years. Fall through it. You are still. On
this migration. We say it is *báiki*, the home we carry within us. Nomadic
peoples. No madness. This migration.

Your traditional clothing consists of_____.

Your National Geographic DNA sequence proves_____.

Part of your history is blank because_____.

You are using that blank stare because <u>*your ancestors could fall into*</u>
<u>*trances.*</u>

## *Jolas*—Tracks made in the snow by reindeer, dogs, or wolves, which have gone in a row

*Men cannot nourish the reindeer, the reindeer must nourish men.*
~ Sámi proverb

Dark with winter,
days pass, hour after hour
on the wolf run.　　There is nothing

you can do, the deer's tendon
is torn from flesh because the wolf held on
and tired the deer, slashed open its neck.

Like the deer, I can only give myself
　　to silence,
to this bloodstained world,
to the violence of our oldest graves

and heed our elders' warning—
You can lose your voice if you
yell too loud at a wolf.

## Njáhcu—Thaw

I name you without words—
    a white scar in stone,
    an island shoreline,
    a footprint in mud.
This is how it comes over me—
like springmelt, like swooning,
like the shadow
pulled back—your own song. wordless.

*Remedy for Unreciprocated Love: Secretly give a small amount of your blood, skin, or sweat to a person to eat to make them fall in love.*

## *Moarri*—Thin ice crust that breaks and cuts the hoofs of horses and reindeers

Sometimes you resurface
with the crack of rifle,

or a knife slice across my forefinger.

If I could stand on an ice floe
in my boots, a seal's blood pooling around me,

I would remember your name.

\*


Space remembers the dead
with antlers, velvet shedding,

the crust on the snow, the spring,
a slick newborn calf.

She is an old map, a glimpse of shoreline.

I remember each windblown skull,
how daylight grips the shadows

flings them into the brittle wind
knowing there is no place here for fragility.

\*

I don't have to be the last
to know about the blood liquid river.

between worlds. I don't have to be
the last to know how to slip through

thinning ice, how to pour blood
into intestines, how to paint the drum

with alder juice, how to listen to the pulse
beneath my own skin.

# Mapping the Drum

Then a magician, spreading out a cloth under
which he might prepare himself for intoning unholy
sorcerers' spells, raised aloft in his outstretched hands
a small vessel similar to a riddle, decorated with tiny
figures of whales, harnessed reindeer, skis, and even
a miniature boat with oars; using these means of
transport the demonic spirit was able to travel across
tall snowdrifts, mountain-sides, and deep lakes.
~ Historia Norwegiae

# Exhibit 422: The Shaman's Drum

Without rock and moss, without the tongue of river, what would I be but merely figures painted in alder blood on skin stretched over the earth. My memory is fashioned from wound—a torn hide transformed from the fire's ashes and bone, from the noose around his neck. They hung my shaman for warming me by the fire, for lying beside him when we traveled to other worlds. Now I cannot return to the mountains, to the half-life of shadowed forest, to the place where he hid me centuries ago. We were all but forgotten and forbidden, yet what priests and collectors did not know is that time is old water, and the wind is still listening. I once had no foothold in this world, no drumstick to tap my way back from this until I noticed when you leaned into this museum case, your skin had mapped his drum before. You are a landscape memory tight-stretched with silhouettes crossing tundra. So listen close: he is still here, dancing on this drumhead, reminding me the stones still have voices, and if the brass ring hits the sign of dawn, we must set out in the morning.

# *Jasa*—Patch of snow in summer or late spring

The sun wanders toward us,
   the window glass still dark,
      my breath frosting air

Spindly birch, earth's bones
   protrude from thin winter hunger
      along the midnight field.

Beneath this rising
   you walked its lighted path,
      a pack on your back.

What do I know of such homecomings—
   I have lost a sense of my own breath
      on the day the sun returns.

# *Spildi*—Very thin layer of ice on water or milk

A weathered calling along this shoreline
is but a throaty rumbling

leaving us to migration—
All along we've been tearstung with chapped faces,

moving through time until we touched
the silver sea with our fingers and hooves,

and we started yoiking and went under
this surface world.

# Likewise Great Observers of Omens

When I left, the tent wall still breathed and night air walked with the bear, the wind was still smokeful. When I left, we were still clans, birds spoke overhead, and I held storms in my fist. Eventually my arms grew tired of breaking through the surface of things. Both sides of the river called out to me, to places where I slipped on slick stones at the edge of two rivers—one cold and full of salmon, the other black and slick with yellow veins and white-lined edges. Somehow I traveled there to the land of lights and more lights. And hungry human herds.

> I shed my skin—
> left it in the middle of a snowy field.
> If you come upon it,
> it will appear to you as a frozen deer hide.

Smoke gives the world sorrow like thin, gray strands of dreams.

Our days are eclipsed by winter, yet, I won't lose sight of one thing—

The land is the oldest grave—our bones sleep restless here.

> I shed my skin—
> Left it in the middle of a snowy field.
> If you come upon it,
> it will appear to you as a coat draping the back of a chair.

Hunger prepares me to prey in darkness, to browse where silence wraps around tented door.

I am warm breath on new-formed ice, snowmelt down your spine. But, no, you say—only a story, a shape

in midnight sun, a jawbone's white gleam on tundra.
Have you forgotten to bury me?

I shed my skin—
left it in the middle of a snowy field.
If you come upon it,
it will appear to you as a blue tarp wrapped across
a broken-down snowmachine, flapping in the wind.

# Oppas—Tracks

The map of my skin—
On my body, the night is star-spun.

A long night sets the hour
of ancient wind.

I keep these old stories
curled in my hands, preparing

for a hungry night like this.

What does it mean
to hold our memories

close enough to brush snow
from winter's sting?

All I know is twilight
still arrives with long tracks,

and a familiar sky scatters
with stars and skin-sting.

This is our center

—skiing across mountaintops,
down valleys, to tundra.

Tell the peculiar thaw

our lives here are small lamps,
slowly melting ice,

and our stories still huddle
over faint flames,

flickering at the center
of the universe: a patch of snow,

toes wiggling the moss
in my boots.

*Suovdnji*—Hole in the snow where ptarmigan hide; grazing hole dug by reindeer; hole dug by humans when melting snow or to shelter from a storm

---

    I should have fixed on
ancient shoals, knowing the difference
between river and sky.

    But our drums, once forbidden,
sleep
in museums' glass cases.
From the curtained window

    our sun hides,
our earth's skin uninhabitable.
Our travels have

    no companions.

*Ulahat*—Almost unrecognizable winter
way or track covered by drifted snow

---

The wolf fades into forest-line
as day tilts toward gray.

The night singer calls from the trees.
Though I love the world cradled in snow,

in the half-light and wind-chatter,
I sense something amiss.

Did you summon the wolf?

or was it just the way he's traveled the familiar,
leaving dust prints on my bedroom floor.

# Stolen by Colonizers: Google Search for Our Sámi Drums

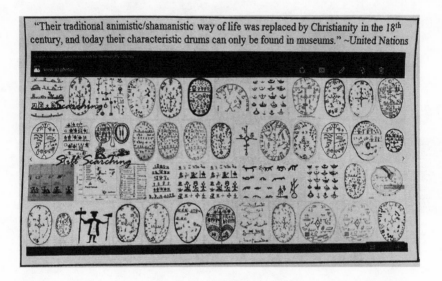

"Their traditional animistic/shamanistic way of life was replaced by Christianity in the 18th century, and today their characteristic drums can only be found in museums." ~United Nations

## Skoavdi—Empty space between snow and the ground

If the ground dances
to its own sound

it must be a shaman lying in grass
and yellow bloom, or a river slipping

between glaciers, a canyon echo,
or perhaps a seaweed-draped tideline.

I can hear it sometimes,
humming animal song

beneath my feet, passing through
my skull. But I cannot answer

a cold prayer.

## *Soatma*—Ice-slush or snow-slush
## on the water of a river or a lake

..................................................................................................................................

*You can't press the wind with a rock.* ~ Sámi proverb

You carry the drumboat—the sewn boat—to the river.
planks stitched. fastened. stitched wood fibers,

clinker fashioned. twist spruce and reindeer sinew thread.
driven needle through bored hole. I am fastened,

and have sewn a running seam. I am of this river-world,
floating down to the lower-world, where our myth's seams

are ripped open. Can you feel the weight of me across your shoulders?

# The Fire Tender

On the shoreline, spirits waited for us—our arrival awoke them.
We saw no tundra, no ice, but weeping trees, a cold drizzle, clouds like
a thick blanket suffocating the expanse. The song they prepared for us
was a slow, deep-throated music inside

our bodies. The steamship plank wobbled under the weight of our
fretting, threatened to plunge us into the unknown. Our suitcases
were heavy in our wet-cold mittened hands. Here is your new home,
they said. Assuring us that worries

are like a bark fire—what looks enormous turns out to be nothing,
really. Come help us dry new wood, compose chants for the thrush
singing up the morning, for the curious seal's bobbing head. So we
gathered by the fire, the familiar place drawing us in,

smudged by the smoke of our promises. Still, we sensed no home
beyond the reach of those flames, no thundering from the under-
world, until an elder held out matches to me, and another held an
armload of wood. This job is for children: Keep putting wood on
the fire, turn the log,

comfort us with hushed words—*dasa dola, dasa dola*—keep the fire
going, keep the fire going. A chant for the fire tender. A chant for the
space wrapping us in its fabric. A chant for the cast-iron stove, and
the peeling framed window, for the small bed in the corner below
the window,

for the pregnant woman sitting there, inhabiting her own fire,
her finger tracing frost on the glass.

## *Goahpálat*—The kind of snowstorm in which the snow falls thickly and sticks to things

What looks like an old woman
    is a snowstorm covering the old stump,

a blue fox parka ruff around her face.
    She is slumped in her old moccasins,

tramping through the field. I imagine her
    hands flattening bread in a pan,

cooking over hot coals, but then her wrinkled
    hands sprout old roots, lichen hair

pokes through the layer of snow.
    How should I greet her?

My palmed hand to warm her face, or a stick
    shaped like a snake left at her feet.

She says, no, you are not simply a passerby,
    —take this memory with you—

# Drum Jingle

Proximity to the edge
of the Pin-of-the-North
there's a waxing moon

and bird path—snow geese
and cranes on a journeying route—
painted runes, bone ring,

antler hammer, metal rings
clinking, clinking. The underside
of this membrane,

is how we used to navigate
this world, holding our future
overhead—drum held to sky,

singing beneath it. Now, how
am I going know when the river
bends toward the sky world?

I am still here dancing on the
rim of sea, picking sea lettuce
from the beach.

Unravel the Wind

# Unleash

We could call up a gale and gust and breeze and storm. We are children of the sun yet rule the wind, a fibrillation of current unwound. We used old songs to claw down trees and pluck gulls from the sky. Our songs were once a secret, handwritten on drum maps, dancing in the half light of the moon. Now, I use the old songs to soothe bees, to call a soft snowfall, for calling up the wind from a scarlet evening sky, for pleas of sailor and sea. We were once shunned, and yes, hung, and stoned, even burned. The rope in our hands—an ancient method to sing up the wind—untying one knot, then two, then three. For singing. They murdered us. For singing.

## *Joavgat*—When falling snow is driven along by the wind

Spun into grief, the wind bends its face,
reaches the open window, and finds my cradle.

I have no memory of drawing in its breath,
or how the old woman wailed,

how she sounded when the ship left
the harbor, sailing for a new land.

I imagine she did not want to dream
that night of her niece's baby,

the child's small fingers wrapping hers.
Now, the memory takes the shape of night,

fills windows with windbreath.
Here, my solitude has teeth,

and riverwind etches snow across
the door. This makes sense, outside

sound moves around the cabin
like a wounded animal.

It, too, wants to let go, to fill the character
of snowthings, to swipe away my scarf

and alight on my collarbone.

# Transgenerationalmigrationallinguistical genocidalinaudiblehistoricalvernacular

Lungs breathe the scent of shore. Stumps and thin trees
are white-skirted. The brightest star is something fragile.
The things I want, the things I have use for, are only words

meant to unravel the wind.

Who knows the joke: After all these centuries,
with expeditions and research, we still do not know
who we are, where we live, how many we are,
and which languages we speak.

Many studies have revealed such wakefulness
as an unblinking owl. We have emerged
from the "dark century."

The official official's office officially states:
"Linguistic genocide can be understood as an end point
on a continuum where the other end point is full enjoyment
of all linguistic human rights."

I ask you, what the nearest thing is to language—
a frosted tongue, the land memory made palatable,
or the river, a dark stitch sewn into earth.

Revitalization and Reclamation: Buy "Learn Saami."
Ships in 3–5 business days. Use Euro Talk.
Download an app. Buy audio bible stories
and lessons: "These recordings are designed
for evangelism and basic bible teaching
to bring the gospel message to people

who are not literate or are from oral cultures,
particularly unreached people groups."

Our Elders say the silent wolf is the real threat.

# *Fáskka*—Snow blown by the wind into an embankment

In the time of stories, they were our food,
and our words were rimmed with knowing ice

Now we suck words from our own marrow,
discover fragments of our bones.

I would rather believe these stories
are our gifts—a woman's hand holding

a worn stone, a brass frog hung
on a string, the pale moon's candle glow.

Let stories hum from your fingertips,
lick them and they'll burn with ice.

Tell stories, like the moon hanging over the sea
across wind-shivered waves. Huddle with them

in cabins and recall them wild like that,
praying to bear skulls cradled in the trees.

## Joðáhat—Tracks in the snow left by a migrating reindeer herd

......................................................................................................

Fractures of moments
    are like a line of skis
where you have come
    and gone.
I listen for the slice of snow
    windspun into music,
but we travel
            away from each other.

## *Veađahat*—Place where snow has been blown away; (nearly) bare patch

I wish I had caught the wings of storms.
I wish I had clung to haloed stars
and water ripples.

That kind of knowing is the one I want.
I want to fling the wheel of fog, pass through
night's window,

and summon the air. I consider
my own lost flight, how my history is littered
with unspeaking.

The wind hunches in the corner.
The wind now has nightmares too.

## *Baahke*—Snow blowing in the wind in warm weather

---

*But the only thing I could accomplish was to get them to utter some atrocious shrieks,*
*in response to which I was forced to stick my fingers*
*in my ears.~ Acerbi (1802)*

The slightest inkling triggered Uncle's voice—
    a guttural sound
like flat stones skipping the lake.

His singing, heard in the distance,
    though no one
said anything about this sin.

And later no one repented.

Nephew stood on the shore, repairing nets,
    heard the songwave
rush the lake, up and down

like his beating heart. He did not stick his fingers
    in his ears, but listened
to the splash of oars,

the pull of song sending him down
    beneath the surface of the lake.

*Joavgama*—Deep snow lying undisturbed
and does not get blown away (in a place
there is shelter from the wind like in a forest)

---

This journey is an ocean current full
of sadness, a prayer of leaving,

two hands offered to the wheel of air.
We shape our own travels by the road

we leave. The old one's marrow dissolves
in my bones from marrying

and marrying and marrying—generations
faint noonlight—Now I hold your lonely bones

up to the light: They are filled with memory.

\*


Our bones are watermarked—a wooden ship's hull
licked with ocean salt, and a wave

through time carries our breath
like a mouthful of cold sea.

We are the light on the surface things,
a whale song pulling us from

this dream. We are the cracked and faded
photo sitting on my desk.

I pick it up and
blow sand from your face.

# Sonnet for Migrations

During the last ice age we were stories, and breath of ice floe, a prayer for light on the outer skin of our bones. The Wind Man shoveled the snow away, and we ventured forth.

Now I must remember there is a space between reindeer tracks, remember we still travel together. My landscape is torn deep here, scarred with glacier teeth, still trying to hold on.

Car lights move like northern lights across bedroom walls. The only wild I know, a siren howl, lights spinning in rearview mirrors.

Like you once did, I wait for migrations of light, for fire to call shadows nearer. I drum you up, strike the taut skin of earth, lift you into the winged place. Our sod house cannot hold you, the smoke hole opens to receive you, and below I wait for the blue light flickering.

Sometimes, I hear you laughing, but maybe it's the wolf cry, howling over our gravesites, or your breath rising through a breathing hole in ice. Or could it be, yes, this infant pressed to my chest.

Night blinks and our breath suspends together over morning frost. Are you listening to wolf licking blood from its paw? Is it our blood? Is it our wolf?

I see a house by the shore, the sea walking toward you where winter is thin, the day longer. You lean between wind and woodpile like a fragile breath that could slip through windows from my world to yours.

I crawl through the membrane, through the door opening between my thoughts and where you sit, wrapped in fur tending bread over fire.

You don't look up but keep warming your hands, keep singing my song in your throat.

Now and then I look in two directions, you drawing me toward your singing, the other, a journey across the sea. I have thought a tree was a man walking toward me. I have thought a city was a stand of trees.

The ocean gathers our voices into ships for the voyage. A better place, they say. A new country, they say. These dreams are full awake, are moving like tide over sea ice, over frail movements of horizon, wobbling with spring rising from earth.

Onboard ship, I hold a wing, broken—no body in sight—just a wing. *Only me, you say, no other travelers on this trail.* My walking stick once poked the earth, steadied me, and led me past swollen rivers, like hooves over stones.

Now, in this new place, I don't know how to read small rocks piled atop one another, or a boulder, its face broken, dotted with moss. Who are these ancestors' spirits in stone?

*There are ways to breathe in this new land, like the summer back home,* you whisper. I inhale mosquitoes. Lick rain. And like an old whale bone sinking into earth, the weight of your thousand years cannot survive the thaw; water pools at my feet, willow roots wrap my ankles. You are gone.

So why, now, do I still unearth a record of these wounds? This time, a fragrant, mossy earthscent in a museum case brightly lit over a soundless drum. I slip from my pocket a treasure kept all these years.

I give this gift for our lost kin, mainly you, a ring of brass to place
on the drum—travel well. Travel well.

And somewhere, eyes like lost words scan valleys and rivers for our
myths—a fragment of antler, a bear skull, a circle of stones.
What survives is your voice hung in the trees.

*Guoldu*—Cloud of snow blowing up
from the ground when there is a hard
frost without very much wind

---

In the distance,
   a bird drinks the sea,
feathers carry no weight.
   Fox sleeps.
Everything is no longer a silhouette.
   I can see them
through this small window.

No one is surprised when

   I lose sight of myself.

*Muohtaborga*—Cloud or spray of snow, either falling or whirled up from the ground by a strong wind

---

Give the wind its breath,
to the sky let it go.

Spin the night world upside down,
toss the docks,

ring ship's bells, tilt the skiff
on its side.

This is how you were meant to be
until the old ones

shed this twilight,
and a familiar voice draws you home.

Traveling to the Sun

## *Doali*—Road or track covered by snow, but still distinguishable

Somewhere I've seen you wake up the sun.
It's like we were old women together

like this before. You and I, back then healing time
while days and nights slipped across our trails.

Beyond the hill, roofs appeared and smoke
curled to clouds.

In our boredom, with our bones creaking,
we tossed stones into the nearby river.

    Like the old proverb says:
    Throwing a stone in the river causes rain.

At the edge of the river—roebay, willowherb,
Jacob's ladder, and monkshood filled the meadow,

poplars flickered gold and green. It rained,
and we turned to each other, leaving us skin-tender.

## *Oavlluš*—Depression or hollow with slushy snow in it, on land or on ice

Do not speak too forceful
with sharp unguarded words,
    especially on the tundra.
Do not call out a greeting.
Do not look back and do not wave.
Never say goodbye.
    Goodbye is forever.
Don't abruptly tell the news from afar,
    but little by little tell us
where the ice has formed a muted space,
and the new ice is so weak it cannot bear us.

*Skávvi*—Crust of ice on snow, formed in
the evening after the sun has thawed
the top of the snow during the day

Here, the edges of stone
are simply our aching knees.
We have been in prayer since
the first human saw the sun.

## *Earpmi*—A little snowfall where the snowflakes are very small

What I hold in my pocket—

leaves like wings imagining sky,
a mossy-headed stone,

a fragment of bone,
a strand of sinew sewn into old red cloth.

I collect these shapes of seasons:
a memory bent into rock,

a wet feather, a glint of glass.
This is how I make sense of letting go—

by holding small things.

# How to say IT

............................................................................................................

say it fast—SÁMI-AMERICAN-AMERICAN-Sámi. Hyphenate.

put some distance between words and generations and peoples

and indigenousness. When they look confused say IT. Grit your teeth but
say IT: LAPP, Lappland, lalalalala. SAY IT then SPIT this "IT" out.

runyourwordstogether:indigenousindigenousUS. Not U.S., as in country,
but as in peoples. Nod when the young woman says she's a white Indian.
Wonder about correcting the corrections and her imperfections and
misconceptions. Say Sámi with an "aw." Sigh when she says her mother
had her eyes done, unfolded and enfolded the epicanthal fold to blend in
with the fold. Her heritage drooping into her line of sight.

Say white-skinned, say light-skinned. Say epicanthal fold and cheekbones.
*Epicanthal folds and oblique palpebral fissures* hypotheses—evolutionary
adaption to harsh winds and snow, **Blepharoplasty** (Greek: ***blepharon***,
"eyelid" + ***plassein*** "to form").

SAY IT. High tone it. Double vowel it. Look IT up on the Internet. Say
Sámi with a Sam-i-am. Say IT like a Saami, like a *saw*, like a cutting
blade, like something you had seen. But you are unseen. Hidden.
Forbidden. Someone said, "Like a white Indian." Someone said,
"I'm 1 percent Sámi." Someone said, "You're not from here." Someone said,
"You are an alien, a real one from outer space." Someone always said, says,
who you are. Define. Classify. Someone said, "You're on the Internet."
Someone stared at you. Someone said nothing. Someone saw nothing.

Say United Nations Declarations. Guide. Affirm. Concern. Recognize.
Welcome. Articles 1 through 46. Theron. Herein. Indigenous. Rights.
Right? Yeah, right.

Say it slooooooooow. Sámi. Say it with your breath. And when IT comes out of your mouth, know this is the first time. Of many times. Enjoy. Feel IT on your tongue. See IT on your face. Mirror, mirror in the hall on the wall, in books, in the dirty looks, in the anthropological notes. Know you are no Joke. Know this is not the last time you will say IT. Write it. Decolonize it. Hold it. A tight embrace is always a fist. Never let it rest. Carry IT across the ocean.

Sámi.

# *Vuožži*—Wet bare ice

The sky wakes as we fly north.
We trace
rivers of black ice,

broken in places,
fanning out, weaving,
brushing riverbanks.

We are birdflock,
wingspans of history
left behind.

Sisters, aunts, cousins, brothers,
flying on hollow winds.
It will always be like this:

A long absence pressing
between us—a single feather
falling from a pale sky.

Our skulls are filled with suns.

# *Loanjis*—Tracks of the whole herd of reindeer

Even at a great distance,
a mother reindeer knows her calf by its grunt.

The sun, cold as a pale moon.
Patches of snow remain. Silence
spreads over the day's bitter teeth.

Even at a great distance, a reindeer calf
knows its mother by her grunt.

Listen—the deer sweep toward us
in a rush of thunder,
the ground vibrates.

# Check the Box

☑

Check only One: African American ☐   American Indian ☐
Alaskan Native ☐   Pacific Islander ☐
Asian American ☐   Hispanic/Latino ☐
White/Off-white/blue-eyed, brown-eyed/epicanthal fold,
no epicanthal fold ☐

Other: YES ☐   NO ☐

Are you a First Homo sapien inhabitant of Europe? YES ☐   NO ☐
Are you a Second-Generation Homo sapien inhabitant of your
American hometown?

YES ☐   NO ☐   If yes: 1st, 2nd, 3rd, 4th, 5th generation

How long have you been separated from your people?
10,000 years ☐   5,000 years ☐
three generations ☐
one year ☐   since dinner ☐

Which traditional garments do you wear?
reindeer moccasins ☐
four-winds hat ☐
gákti ☐
Carhartts ☐
feathered headdress ☐
Do you know how to ski? YES ☐   NO ☐
Can you ride a horse? YES ☐   NO ☐

Can you steal a horse? YES ☐   NO ☐

Have you ever butchered a reindeer? YES ☐  NO ☐
   Explain:
Have you ever ridden a reindeer? YES ☐  NO ☐
Do you play the drum? YES ☐  NO ☐

Do you sing weird songs without words in the woods?
YES ☐  NO ☐  I resist the urge ☐

Does your blood contain mtDNA subhaplogroup U5b?
YES ☐  NO ☐

Or mtDNA haplogroup V? YES ☐  NO ☐

Do you identify yourself as something old and discarded,
a scrap of clothing?
YES ☐  NO ☐

Have you ever heard of a Noaide? YES ☐  NO ☐
Can you call a whale to shore? YES ☐  NO ☐
Do you really think you came from the Sun? YES ☐  NO ☐

# Gaska-geardi—Layer of crust

Like a long winter's story
    she spoke with edges of sharp ice.
I didn't know it then
    but she had come to rename me,
rid me of a colonizer's sleep.

She shook loose the membrane,
    and brass bells called me forth
like a loon through riverweeds.
    *From the whirlpools*, she called out,
*from the slick river rocks,*
    *from the gray, silt-filled space,*

*come running now.*

# Write like a Sámi

Be in-di-gen-ous. Write about ancestors, one whose face is weathered, wise, and old. Not your old-short-fat-great-grandpa farming fish in ponds in his backyard.

Write like you're a Sámi. Write about drums. Not the imitation drum you ordered online because your sun-cross travels in all directions and you don't know how to heat bend, or how to draw the realm of gods.

Reference the northern lights. Don't write about plate glass and structural steel but tundra and lavvus. Maybe get a Sámi name. You remember how they colonized you, took away your name and gave you another one. Find a Bath Mother willing to wash it away with boiled alder bark. Call yourself something exotic—the page will take notice of Ráijá or Biehtár.

Your prose or poem must mention reindeer, or perhaps a noiade traveling with the underground people; their feet against ours, pressing up toward the surface of this world.

Make sure you reveal and divulge and disclose you're a Sámi or they'll think you're New Agey. Call up the spirits when you do: Good spirits, bad spirits, drunk spirits, and good-bad-drunks—relatives who floated facedown, tangled in a fishing boat's rigging,

cousins who tumbled and rolled in pickup trucks from the highway to the beach below. And mention the spirits peering up from a birch wood cup— the readers and the double-checkers will anticipate this with their hands rubbed together and their head nods and an *ah-ha* rigid against their palates.

Mention yoiks.

Write like a Sámi. Refer to raising the wind and smearing butter on your doorframe and tin thread dragged through a die with your teeth. But leave out Y chromosomal polymorphisms and translucency of the iris— you know where that'll lead.

# *Ukiuq*—Become winter

**skilĐi** (North Saami)
> Covering of little bits of ice that hangs down loosely
> on rough fabric, or on fur with the hair on, or in the hair or beard.

**qaqiqsurniq** (Aivilik Inuit)
> Small pillar-like protrusions of snow formed after the soft
> or less-compacted snow around animal tracks
> has been eroded by a blizzard.

**tjilla** (Lule Saami)
> A hole or cave dug in the snow by birds or small animals
> to stay warm and sheltered.

**lunta** (Finnish)
> Snow.

**elakaq ukiuq** (Yupik)
> The hole in the ice has got water in it/the person making the hole
> in the ice finally chipped all the way through the ice,
> permitting the hole to fill with water.

**magesnø** (Norwegian)
> Snow all the way up to the stomach.

**kujjiniq** (Aivilik Inuit)
> Hole melted in the sea ice by a foreign object
> such as seaweed or a pebble.

**isknolde** (Danish)
> Rounded formations of ice in saltwater
> often attached to other ice.

**aɣiuppiniq** (Greenlandic Inuit)
    Wave-like snow drift on frozen sea or inland ice
        caused by the wind.

**uqaluraq** (Inuktitut)
    An eroded soft snow mound resembling a tongue.

**bergy bit** (English)
    Large chunk of glacier in the sea.

**mau** (Eastern Canadian Inuit)
    Small ice floe that sinks when one steps onto it.

**hengefonn** (Norwegian)
    A snowdrift hanging on the side of a rock
        or having a shape like the bow of a ship.

**paiXciq** (Alutiiq)
    Be a snowstorm.

**upplega** (Swedish)
    Snow collected in the trees
        when it snows a lot without any wind.

**mingullaut** (Inuktitut) (Aivilik Inuit)
    Fine, powdery snow that sifts in through cracks,
        or settles on objects.

**kusukaq** (Central Siberian Yupik)
    Glaciated spot where water has dripped
        and frozen to the ground.

**iniruviit** (Inuktitut)
> Joints or cracks in the ice that open and close
> > continuously like hinges during high and low tides,
> > but do not shift sideways.

**tjalhvaldahkesne** (South Saami)
> For a dog to be full of icicles.

# A Dark Imagining

# All the Sámi Findings

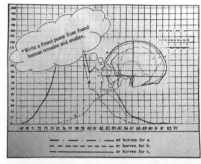

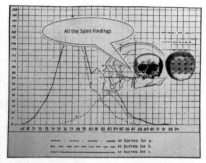

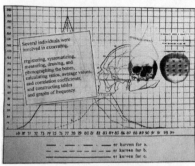

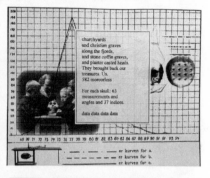

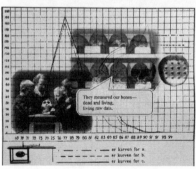

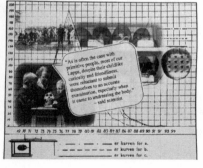

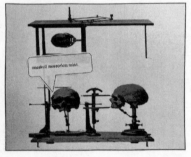

## *Bulltje*—Large lumps of snow that stick to a house

It was as if the bear
was an old woman who turned her face from me.

She sat on the porch bumbling through a box.
I peered from the other side of the window, hidden from sight.

She chose a silver can, a scrap of bread,
chewed the marrow of bone.

For a moment, I considered that I could
bring her back from winter's thicket,

from the windblown edge of earth.
I could've done it with a song,

perhaps a story carved heavy with old roots and bog.

Instead, I pulled the space between us closer—
pressed my face to the glass, sensed

an open door and collapsing walls,
and conjured a silk scarf for her shoulders

and a silver trinket for her wrist.

# Imagine not knowing if you're a man or a reindeer

····································································································

Your favorite coat is covered in hollow hairs, and there's a dense network of blood vessels in your nose, and you never sweat. You love being social, and you're a vegetarian, You love sledding and traveling, and you're an avid runner, and you're always carrying someone else's burden.

Your white velvet suit is your favorite.

You're convinced there's an air sack in your neck lifting your tenor voice, and you shuffle your feet and look down when talking. You've always avoided predators in the dark. You love the scent of muskeg, though you avoid it because there's an overwhelming urge to lounge among the tundra tea.

Every cell in your body is sensitive, and you scatter your light every-where you go. People notice some days your eyes appear blue and other days they look gold. But, recently, you've noticed a change—You used to have great night vision, and winter was your favorite season.

Now you've been using those eyes to cope with winter's darkness, and wavelengths of light appear bent in strange ways, which could be related to pressures and stresses. Work has been tough, and the sun feels like it's always below the horizon. You wonder if your adaptation and use of winter light has always been a dim illusion.

Occasionally your hair grows shaggy, and you resist the desire to rub your head against the doorframe. But you're still good at tending your house plants—your dwarf shrub and succulent window garden is fabulous. Lately, though, when the stars are chasing through the sky and you're out strolling your neighborhood at night, you can still feel Grandmother— even though she's gone now—patting your head and calling you *Ravddat, reindeer, which keeps itself to the edge of the herd.*

## *Njeađgga*—Ground drift: drifting snow blown up from the ground, covering roads or tracks

I know a woman who glides on ice,
red-faced from breathing time.

She sings the evening, the morning,
another night. She makes spirits flee

leaving traces of ice fog—But tonight,
I cannot sleep beneath her half-closed eyes.

Instead, I listen to the slow spilling night,
to the hole in the world

where moon and silver river slip through.
This is where I see you, Auntie,

sitting on the riverbank, weaving grass
for our shoes.

No one can imagine you here, they say. I can.

# White Reindeer's Skull Is the Sky

My weeping, my pleading, my begging did not stop him.
No law then to prevent him from doing this thing I cannot
give voice to except as creation story—

*White Reindeer laid down on emptiness.*

He forced himself into sacred hollow places, where old
women had gathered for generations within me,

*From White Reindeer's body, veins opened up*

traces of them still sloughed into crevasses, still etched on
inner walls with lichen.

*and blood streamed out, transforming into rivers.*

He clenched his teeth and whispered in my ear: whore,
bitch, cunt, adulterer, mine, did he do it to you like this?

*The White Reindeer's stomach churned and gurgled*
*and poured out and became the ocean.*

Afterward he paraded me in front of my parents,
my teenage body and mind still wandering circles on tundra.

*The White Reindeer's horns fell off and the horns grew up*
*tall and became mountains.*

The shape and shame of me traveled from animal to earth,
knowing story-instinct has followed other women like me before,

*Then the reindeer's fur grew into trees and grass,*

women telling these same stories, emerging from
beneath logs, from a palm holding a plucked leaf,
from scraping across glaciers, falling from the sky, even.

*and the White Reindeer's skull became the sky.*

Sometimes when I close my eyes, all these years later,
I see stars and northern lights in the reindeer's eyes

*The eyes of the reindeer became the constellations—*

and I'm able to compress my fibers, and my small bones
fuse together, and I'm there as the world began, my story
sliced open and flowing.

## *Siivu*—The going; the state of the ground for traveling, the travel conditions

This is how to travel to the land of the dead:
Put an ax in your coffin, a flint striker

and stone, a bow and arrow. Rise up
on the last day. You will need a torch

to find your way. Hack the trees with your ax.
Burn them down if you must.

Find your way to the dwelling of the blessed
with your ax in hand, bending light.

# Anthroapology

sorry, sorry, sorry.

They said. unlawful intervention. and human rights. right?
But necessary work. well preserved. unique possibilities.
They will keep our bones safe. Safe. wellLit. Secure.
preserved. thank you, Giitu. kind find. Refind that you are.
They measured, pulled the DNA from flesh and bone and stone
and the molecules that carried us spilled out
Results, fragments, instructions in our cells:

> Take no notice of wind
> or sun, but reindeer hooves weaving
> a path between valleys.
> Follow it
> until you discover
> the fire is cold
> and only a ring of stones remain.

Tracks are dreams pressed into spines—walked up our backs and
down our legs, our long strands spiraling. We have been a wolf.
hereditary material.

This world is well-fed: fish migrate
to deep water, bears gorge on berries,
marmots fill holes with pine nuts
and currants, reindeer eat mushrooms.

The Wind is the rungs cutting our skin shallower here. I sense
sharpness beneath my skin: a memory bent into rockshapes.

> We wade the sea. salt salt salt.
> Brine in your food and in our bodies.
> Our bodies are pale suns. Time perches on the bow
> of our skiffs and our paddle strokes slice the sea.

And us.

We are so long that we can't fit into our own cells. We are tightly
coiled. 23 pairs of hollow hairs. You study my bones and discover
layers of fur, a woolly undercoat. Our bones breathe cold air and
cool the arteries around our hearts.

How we inhabit the world: Our lives are nets full of birds
I unfold light, return winter
and ourselves.
Tufts of reindeer hair press into mud.

This place is a constant hum. Maybe you can see I am backlit, and I
am still breathing last night's dream

and all I can do is borrow a lamp
for the long journey back home.
It has been a long journey, indeed.

DNA Material returned. Us. Historical value = 9,000 years. We
divide and copy ourselves, and transform. We are newborn calves
walking in spring snow.

# Observant

Tell us how your sight has more teeth than ours, your gold streets
and deliverance give us more hope.

Our antlered heads are our histories—blood-filled and velvet covered.
There is no way to separate ourselves

from the deer, or the snow dusting brittle ice. They link and interlink.
How can I tell you this river between realms is not just a myth,

but a story holding me in all worlds.

The story is hung beside the tent in a stretched hide. I keep it
padded with moss because it is our fragility.

I keep this story from breaking open. I can disrobe it like skin
and like a sun-bleached rag; I hang it in the trees.

Some days I hang it low in the branches or toss it up into the alpine
meadow. Some days I lift it high over my head, a ceremony to the sky.
No one knows what is inside the skin.

I don't tell. They only guess—they tease me: a tuft of reindeer hair,
two silver salmon scales, the north wind, a pinch of coffee grounds,
and perhaps a pencil.

Yes, I say, all of those are my hallowed lives.

*Driving Wolves Away: Cut a square out of a fresh wolf snow print and recite an incantation.*

## Šalka—Firm, hard, winter way; hard-trodden snow on yard, a marked-place

He reshaped the moon
bit it—chewed light—

played with what remained,
flicked it around

with his tail, tossed it into a pond.
Wolf,

why can't you just leave me alone?
You lure me from this windowsill

with your nightly chant, leaving teeth marks
on my spiny-edged dreams.

*Roavku*—Portion of water (river, lake, marsh) or frozen bank, waterside (near a spring), where the ice has formed in such a way that there is a hollow space under the top layer

---

    Freezing is benign as the air crumbles with grief
and I can sense hollow spaces
    beneath my first layer of skin,
knowing our knowledge is necessary
    for baring our weight into generations,
things I cannot yet see.
    I blow warm breath on my hands, step lightly.
If my fingers could speak
    they would tell the shape of ice
like the tips of wings touching air.
    I touch as if to expand sky
and summon the world open—
    can't you see this, what's happening?
I listen for voices, meet silence with old snow,
    fingers untuck from fingers—
the ice is forming.
    This could mean the lining
of delicate things still understands
    hard frost without wind,
where the ice does not form,
    and where ice forms when the reindeer flock
has stayed for a while in mild weather.

She is not a myth but a dark imagining. She is a dull murmur in the trees
where the wind is praying its sorrowful primal story. But how does this
story begin—with either the windswept tundra, or here on this bridge
hovering over Sitka's harbor. Beyond, there is no snowpack on the
mountains this year. They say the world is melting. She knows how
it feels to melt. She walks across the bridge to the coffee shop below.
She stirs the black sky in her coffee. Her ancestors once stirred starlight.
She opens her laptop and searches for her anthropological self,
her ancestral self, her historical self, her assimilated self. Skridfinn, Saami,
Sámi, North Sámi, South Sámi, Mountain Sámi, Sea Sámi. Sometimes she is
two seconds away from her people. Or 3,458 miles. Whichever is easier.
Whichever fits into this global revolving hypertext markup language spin.
Sitka, Alaska, to Gáivuotna-Kåfjord, Norway: No Routes Found. Except
she is a charged particle like the spirits in the aurora—she uses Google Earth.
She is ever-present but appears and disappears, high altitude atomic oxygen
colliding, turning red. She wonders how many grandmothers and aunties
and cousins you can search for, back-and-forth in time, before the shoe-bands
of your world weaken. And below a woman stands alone, chanting in the
morning's depth symmetry, sliding in and out of pitch, tightening her throat,
her notes leaping up and down.

*Čuohki*—Ice sheet formed by rain on open ground that subsequently freezes; this causes the worst grazing as the reindeer are unable to dig down to the lichen

---

I gave a bead as a gift,
and danced among birches.

But, no, this was not me
but a grandmother,

an aunt, a root of tree.
The sun has left us

to carry these stories
like a wind brittle branch.

# The Tent Wall Still Breathes

# *Boara*—During spring when the ice melts on a river and ice-slush is gushing out

*You spoke perfect Norwegian, translated fluently to Sami in church and when the
sheriff, clergyman, or other authority figure descended upon sinners of various kinds.*
~ Aagot Vinterbo-Hohr

At the end of winter,
I mend nets—language tangled
with salmon.

Words rip through my fibers.
The river, still frozen,
breaks into a thousand ice shards

and the net sways beneath
silty green water.
We have forgotten how

to say: "winter steady,"
"fatty salmon," and "that which goes down
to the sea in the spring
and returns again in the autumn."

Our words are lost
within this late season,
in that slow, deep place,

in this small river of me,
where my mouth still feels
the pull of bonehook.

*Ainnádat*—When snow has covered the (ski/animal) tracks but they are still slightly visible

Like skipping flat stones,
I toss my voice across water—
an echo of wild sorrow.

They say sometimes a herder
can hear another's song.
It's carried on the wind,

and journeys through
to the edge of this shore.

\*

Movement—we pause for tangled harnesses, packs slipping,
animals flicking dwarf birch. We descend, clatter over white,
round stones, sweep over ridges, rivers curve sharp with spring flood.
Slipstream drives snow into our faces. We float over glossed ice,
scrape through openings in poplar. Branches fling back; snow spatters
our faces.

# Observations of the Lapp Jaw

Traveler, trace my face. Lean in. Press your head to mine. Measure
me between finger and thumb. I open and close. After we finish, you
write something in your notebook. What? I see questions in your eyes.
Where do you come from? We've had travelers here before. Some in
the daytime, others follow darkness, pursuing the exotic. You say I
have protomorphic peculiarities and consider a turned-up nose, short
stature, projecting cheekbones.

Notes: Four races
1. white
2. yellow
3. black
4. lapplander

A branch of a white-yellow ur-race. Homopaleoarcticus. Homohyper-
boreus. Hyperbrachycephalic. As the glaciers receded, we developed
fine-headed hair. We are local shrunken Paleolithic survivors. In the
village, we lined up for measurements and you paused when you saw
me. I raised my head slightly. Didn't want to look you in the future.
I slipped the two small oranges you gave to me into my coat pocket.
Your fingers and figures showed the average female Lapp to have a
cranial capacity of 1300.87 cc compared to an average female Europe-
an capacity of 1300 cc.

More notes:
1. well set limbs
2. black hair
3. broad face
4. stern countenance
5. laziness
6. sorcery
7. temper

8. dirty clothes
9. in possession of drums and stallos

Low stature; tawny (swarthy) complexion; extremely lean; thick heads and prominent foreheads; hollow and blare eyed; short, flat noses; wide mouths; flat faced; meager cheeks; long chin; short, thin, straight, black hair; thin and short beard; strong and active; stooped walk; superstitious, timerous, and cowardly: unfit for soldiery.

Years later, in the churchyard, you accompany the priest and two hired hands, digging up a grave. A fine specimen. You put the box in the cart along with the others. And back at the university maybe you sighed—maybe you didn't—when the measurements determined my forehead low and slanting; head squared in form; the lateral projection of my malars.

On the same plane of my malar bones, I swept you forward a few hundred years. And she is in the classroom reading your notes, because the universities of everywhere expected this. Skulls stack the shelves behind her, some with mouths partially open, some with broken and chipped jaws. And more jaws: Jaws with and without skulls, a jaw whose last word still empties forth, a jaw that kissed the space between a newborn's fontanelle, a jaw that sang the moose horns protruding from the riverbank, a jaw that brushed a pubis.

Her stomach is upset whenever she enters this room with you. She is expected to be objective by the objectification. She wants to make paper airplanes with your notes. The professor goes on and on about how apparent it is that Bryn, Czekanowski, and von Eickstedt have only partially accepted the hypothesis of Stratz, Lassila, and Kajava And there it comes again, the urge to spin around the room, to hover above it. She recalls your annotations, the reason you claim her people are fainthearted is that excessive cold and miserable diet renders their blood destitute of a sufficient quality of spirits. So she raises her hand to her face and notes scarcely any superciliary ridges, taps her narrow nasal entrance.

That afternoon she makes love with her girlfriend on their wet porch, a blue quilt spread out across the hard-planked wood. She stares up at the cottonwood leaves falling, as her girlfriend's face is haloed in September light. She blinks as leaves tumble and turn into research notes and then back again.

She smells oranges, but she lives on an island in Alaska and the weekly shipment of oranges has missed the barge. Wet leaves stick to her back and slowly her malar fossa forms a slight excavation, and when the alveolar edge of her jaw arches in front, she knows that she knows— due to the natural evolution of her type, brought about during a long seclusion in a changed environment, her chin is rather prominent.[1]

---

1 Her evaluation of the Lapp jaw is still a footnote.

# *Ritni*—Rime on trees and other things (thick)

If you believe
you have a wound

that holds blue light in a feathery form,
believe that

the cold is unprepared for your throaty singing,
the night doesn't recognize you.

How is it we lost the ability to do this?
There is no evidence of wounds—

no scars on the larynx,
no swollen tongue.

But what happens when one language
is replaced by another,

when we can no longer sing the fog
freezing to the windward

side of the branch?
Our skulls now flatten as images

sketched in anthropologists' notebooks.
Our skin cells swell with fear.

Our flesh is tucked down
between lichen-covered stones.

## *Lavki*—Slippery going; ice covered with loose, dry snow with no foothold

Who would know that whales pass here

so close they look you in the eye,
that whale and human bones

lie here side by side, our ribs enjoined beneath
a star-spackled sky, our ghost skulls full of wind—

Their memories chant back at us,
reminding us how everything speaks of loss.

# Survival Skills

If you wander through midsummer
believing in spirits grown old,
the summer fog smoothing the sea,

Raven dipping his wings,
    hinting at ancient cracks in the world—

perhaps you can silence this
longing, this chanting of hollows,
shift the stretching light.

Perhaps you can walk to my door
and take me with you—
there is a crust on the snow

not strong enough for carrying humans.

# *Bihci*—Rime (frost)

We held the first frost, welcomed fading light,
the trail cracking with the weight of us.

I think of you now, breaking ice, the cabin
morning-cold, lighting a small lamp.

I want to say to you—you are still here,
still beloved, still living,

because my father eats with the edge of his knife.

*Srevlla*—The state of things where the
spring snow is so soft that one sinks into it

The fire holds our eyes
to the long silence. Sparks flicker,

mosquitoes buzz. The smoke-lulled night
sulks beside snowmelt.

I am reminded of this season of bluedark,
where our hush dresses us with breath.

And when we speak this way around the fire,
in the knowing, without words—

We must wait until the night bird calls us back into story
and returns us to our hollow-backed selves.

# Šlahta—Rainy, wet snow or sleet

Relative, some afternoons disappear
with rain's hiss and pummel,

loosening soil and tempers, wearing
away trails and footholds.

I want to sit in the terrible dark
without refuge, with maybe

some grub and raincoat,
beneath a weeping

hemlock among water-strewn roots.
This is how I enter your world,

five generations back, a thin-threaded
network of points and directions,

illustrated like an ancient divination
on a nautical compass.

There I will find you, summoning me
in the wind's coil, intoning Granddaughter,

listening close to that old hymn of earth,
enchanted as a midday squall.

# *Gavdda*—Thin ice, bay (or young) ice

I will never move over shoreline
like a stormbird
pressing wings to current.

I am still in the skinboat
beside the cliff
etching Woman-with-a-Bow in rock walls.
This might be the last of our fragile story.

# Across the Drum Skin

The light is late when color fades all to sleep
and I sit by my firepit as thoughts drum up

other thoughts and smoke rises to awaken
the Pin-of-North and I am here thinking

of sieve drum and burl drum formed
from trees growing with the sun.

   *skin from a year-old doe*

But there is a membrane world I cannot breach
and I'm thousands of miles from my ancestral home.

   *red boiled alder bark, or reindeer blood*

As I watch the flames, I sense my skin is thinning
and I fan away smoke and pet my dog.

Somewhere there's a drum
with a sky hunter and he's ready

at any moment to shoot down the polar star.
Thoughts tumble in with the flames

and I wonder if I'm a Sámi knockoff
like the dolls in the window of an Arctic shop

or a cartoon gakti.

   Someone is selling my spirit on eBay again—
Am I the tourist drum on my wall or the touristy four-winds hat?

My sealskin boots leave no trace, so am I really real?
I am not a sacrificial altar for anyone lately,

but carved lines are shadows shaping a bird-path
across my arms, and there are fish, wolves,

reindeer, snake, bear, beaver, and eagles leaping
through flames, ready to assist this journey.

   *wisdom revealed on the skin of a female deer*

The flames lick back toward themselves, shaping
an *Oval* and at that moment I know

my People-of-the-Sun knew the earth
bulged like an oval in her orbit.

Now to convince myself—what I hear
is a woodpecker tapping the spruce tree

behind me, or maybe a grouse on the hillside
in the dark, thump, thump, thumping his chest.

# To Be Found Due to Tracks

*An Arctic Peoples' snow dictionary poem*

The first film of ice forming along tidal flats,
When the sides of a river freezes, and when rocks
    freeze to the ground,
Ice on a river.

To come new snow,
Water drops cooled to freezing,
Light snow with distance between snowflakes.

Snow as fine as dust,
Small puddles of water in snow,
Ice formed at the flow edge
    when snow-soaked water freezes.

Water in a river freezing in a waterfall
    and building up to a considerable thickness,
Fine spicules or plates of ice—suspended in water,
Ice-bridge or snow-bridge over a river.

The ice is now travelable; it will hold a person,
Hunting on moving ice,
Wave-like snow drifts on frozen sea.

A seal breathing hole,
Indentation in floe ice,
Circular ice pans with a rough edge.

Ice along the shore of open water,
Sea ice attached to icebergs, glaciers, or shore,
White glare on the underside of clouds,
  indicating presence of ice: an ice blink.

A piece of ice coming like a foot,
Hard footprint,
Snow that falls down into the shoes.

To walk on thin ice,
Transparent ice on water,
Ice moving with currents.

Blue-like transparent ice,
Cross open water by jumping from floe to floe,
Slippery ice underneath a layer of snow.

Narrow edge of ice,
Ice formed on top of ice, creating pressure ridges,
Crack within a crack.

A place to cross,
A crack in the ice that opens, freezes, and then reopens,
A crack you have to jump over to cross.

A pause between two falls of snow.
Winter-movement road,
Fresh tracks.

Windblown snow at the place
  of feeding reindeers,
A hollow space between the ground

and the snow,
When the skis sink deep.

Old, even drifted snow, which can bear,
    up in the mountains,
A narrow path after an avalanche,
Snow all the way to the belt.

A rounded formation in a snowdrift,
A cave dug by humans in snow,
Female polar bear's den in snowdrift.

Animal tracks covered by snow,
Wind with snow,
To throw loose snow on someone.

Old snow that looks like coarse grains of salt,
Porridge-like ice,
Snowdrift—tongue shaped.

Black frost,
A Winter night,
A crack that is widening.

The ice sings or the ice is making sounds,
The sounds of cracking in the trees due to cold,
Pearls of ice frozen to lichen.

Crossing old tracks in the snow,
Old skiing track that is difficult to follow,
Creak from footsteps in snow.

A skiing track that stops,
Untouched winter snow without tracks,
Sink into soft ground or snow.

Ice crystals that seem to float in the air,
Snow that a person will fall through,
A shaman's word for snow.

# Remedy for Assimilation

Press a bear's tooth or reindeer jawbone
    on the affected area of the tooth. Learn

to pull poems from your bones.
    Massage your head and neck and tug hair

at the apex of your head, and wash
    your head in hot coffee to heal a headache.

Inhabit the memory of the last ice age.
    Have a bag ready to bury with yourself:

It should contain a blue ink pen; dry shoe-hay;
    a smooth, round stone; a small notebook.

Leave an offering of reindeer carcasses,
    fish fat and other precious objects at sacred sites

for good luck. Rub corn snow on frostbite.
    Recite an incantation while rubbing a frog

on infected skin. Re-center and re-enter
    identity in this stretch of the river. Recreate

your story to be told to outsiders. Recognize
    collective memory—see your face

carved in a tree. Hang meat in its branches,
    smear it with grease.

# Notes

*Sámi is sometimes spelled Saami. Sámi were once called *Lapp*, which is a derogatory term.

vii riddle: A *lavvu* is a Sámi tipi/tent. The "Old Woman" is the tent itself, the "berries" are the fire's coals, and the Old Woman's lap is the "center" of the lavvu where the fire is located.

10 "A Thousand Words for Snow": Northern Sámi language. The Sámi are the one hundred thousand Indigenous inhabitants of Norway, Sweden, Finland, and the Russian Kola Peninsula. There are more than thirty thousand Sámi living in the United States.

19 "*Njáhcu*—Thaw." A *yoik* is the traditional Sámi chant and is sometimes wordless. The North Sámi language has hundreds of words for snow conditions.

20 "Remedy for Unreciprocated Love: Secretly give a small amount of your blood, skin, or sweat to a person to eat to make them fall in love" is from "Johan Turi's animal, mineral, vegetable cures and healing practices: an in-depth analysis of Sami (Saami) folk healing one hundred years ago," by Thomas A. DuBois and Jonathan F Lang, *Journal of Ethnobiology and Ethnomedicine* 9, no. 57 (2013). https://doi.org/10.1186/1746-4269-9-57.

25 "Exhibit 422: The Shaman's Drum," is a Noiade drum confiscated from Anders Poulsen in 1691.

27 "*Spildi*—Very thin layer of ice on water or milk," depicts a *yoik*, which is Sámi chanting/throat singing.

65 "*Vuožži*—Wet bare ice," is a term in the Lule and North Sámi language.

73 "*Ukiuq*—Become winter," the poem's title is Inupiaq.

92 "*Roavku*—Portion of water (river, lake, marsh) . . . ," last line is from the North Saami dialect, Čilvi: where ice forms when the reindeer flock has stayed for a while in mild weather.

97 "*Boara*—During spring when the ice melts on a river and ice-slush is gushing out," is one of the hundreds of words for snow in the North Sámi language.

99 In "Observations of the Lapp Jaw," the footnote is part of the poem.

For language and culture assistance, I consulted the following books and articles:

Anderson, Robert T. "Lapp Racial Classifications as Scientific Myths." *Anthropological Papers of the University of Alaska* 11, no. 1 (1962).

Beach, Hugh. *A Year in Lapland*. Seattle: University of Washington Press, 2001.

DuBois, Thomas A., and Jonathan F. Lang. "Johan Turi's animal, mineral, vegetable cures and healing practices." *Journal of Ethnobiology and Ethnomedicine* 9, no. 57 (August 2013). http://www.ethnobiomed.com/content/9/1/57.

Gaski, Harald, ed. *In the Shadow of the Midnight Sun: Contemporary Sami Prose and Poetry*. Karasjok: Davvi Girji OS, 1997.

Gaup, Eira, Inger Marie, Christian Jaedicke, Olde Herik Magga, and Nancy Maynard et al. "Traditional Sámi Snow Terminology and Physical Snow Classification: Two Ways of Knowing." *Cold Regions Science and Technology* 85 (January 2013): 117–30. doi.org/10.1016/j.coldregions.2012.09.004.

Hatt, Emilie Demant. *With Lapps in the High Mountains: A Woman among the Sami, 1907–1908.* Translated by Barbara Sjoholm. Madison: University of Wisconsin Press, 2013.

Helander, Elina, and Kaarina Kailo. *No Beginning, No Ending: The Sami Speak Up.* Circumpolar Research Series No 5. Alberta: Canadian Circumpolar Institute; Kautokeino Norway: Nordic Sami Institute, 1998.

Jackson, Sheldon. *Annual Report on Introduction of Domestic Reindeer into Alaska.* Ann Arbor: University of Michigan Library, 1898.

Jensen, Ellen Marie. *What We Believe In: Sami Religious Experience and Beliefs from 1593 to the Present.* Karasjok: CálliidLágádus/Authors' Publisher, 2015.

———. *We Stopped Forgetting: Stories from Sámi Americans.* Karasjok: CálliidLágádus/ Authors' Publisher, 2012.

Kulonen, Ulla-Maija, Irja Seurujärvi-Kari, and Risto Pulkkinen. *The Saami: A Cultural Encyclopedia.* Helsinki: The Finnish Literary Society, 2005.

Laestadius, Lars Levi. *Fragments of Lappish Mythology.* Translated by Borje Vahamaki. Edited by Juha Pentikainen. Beaverton, ON: Aspasia Books, 2002.

Magga, Ole Henrik. "Diversity in Saami Terminology for Reindeer, Snow, and Ice." *International Social Science Journal* 58, no. 187 (December 2006):25–34. https://doi.org/10.1111/j.1468–2451.2006.00594.x.

Omniglot. "North Sámi Language, Alphabet and Pronunciation." Updated April 23, 2021. https://omniglot.com/writing/northernsami.htm.

Pentikainen, Juha. "The Shamanic Drum as Cognitive Map." *Cahiers de Littérature Orale. Open Edition Journals.* January 2010. https://journals.openedition.org /clo/445.

Riseth, Jan Age, Hans Tommervik, Eliza Helander-Renvall, and Niklas Labba et al. "Sámi Traditional Ecological Knowledge as Guide to Science: Snow, Ice and Reindeer Pasture Facing Climate Change." *Polar Record* 47, no. 3 (July 2011). doi.org/10.1017/S0032247410000.

Rydving, Hakan. *The End of Drum Time: Religious Change Among the Lule Saami, 1670s–1740s.* Historia Reigionum, No 12. Uppsala Universitet, 2nd edition, 2004.

Scheffer, Johannes. *The History of Lapland, wherein are shewed the original, manners, habits, marriages, conjurations, & of that people.* Project Gutenberg. Released June 7, 2019. https://www.gutenberg.org/files/59695/59695-h/59695-h.htm.

Sexton, Randall, and Ellen Anne Buljo Stabbursvik, "Healing in the Sami North." *Culture Medicine and Psychiatry* 34 (December 2010), 571–89. doi.org/10.1007 /s11013-010-9191.

Took, Roger. *Running with Reindeer: Encounters in Russian Lapland.* New York: Basic Books, 2005.

Vitebsky, Piers. *The Reindeer People: Living with Animals and Spirits in Siberia.* New York: Mariner Books, Houghton Mifflin Harcourt, 2005.

Wallin Weihe, and Hans Jorgen. *Snow and Ice: What Has Always Been Known.* Lillehammer: Permafrost Press, 2006.

# About the Author

VIVIAN FAITH PRESCOTT was born and raised in Wrangell, in Southeastern Alaska. She lives in Wrangell at her family's fishcamp. She's of Sámi, Norwegian, Finnish, German, and Irish heritage, and others. She is a member of the Pacific Sámi Searvi. She was adopted by the T'akdeintaan, her children's clan, and given the name Yéilk' Tlaa. She's married to poet and retired Coast Guardsman Howie Martindale and has four children, two stepchildren, nineteen grandchildren, and four great-grandchildren. She holds an MA in cross-cultural studies with an emphasis in Indigenous knowledge systems, an MFA in poetry from the University of Alaska, and a PhD in cross-cultural studies from the University of Alaska, Fairbanks.

She is the author of two full-length poetry collections, *Silty Water People* (Cirque Press, 2020) and *The Hide of My Tongue* (Plain View Press, 2012), and five poetry chapbooks, *Slick* (White Knuckle Press, 2010), *Sludge* (Flutter Press, 2012), *Our Tents Are Small Volcanoes* (Quills Edge Press, 2017), *Traveling with the Underground People* (Finishing Line Press, 2018), *The Last Glacier at the End of the World* (Split Rock Press, 2020), a short story collection, *The Dead Go to Seattle* (Boreal Books/Red Hen Press, 2017), and a foodoir, *My Father's Smokehouse* (West Margin Press/Alaska Northwest Books, 2022). She is a two-time recipient of a Rasmuson Fellowship (2015, 2019) and a recipient of the Alaska Literary Award (2017). Her work has been nominated for Pushcart Prizes and Best of the Net. Her nonfiction appears in an award-winning column called Planet Alaska in the *Juneau Empire*. Her website is vivianfaithprescott.com and you can find her on Twitter at planet_alaska and poet_tweet.